Chainsaw Carving
an EAGLE

BY JAMIE DOEREN
AND DENNIS ROGHAIR

Fox
Chapel Publishing

1970 Broad Street • East Petersburg, PA 17520
www.FoxChapelPublishing.com

Dedication

To Bev, to Amber and Zachary, and to Lisa who has helped in more ways than she knows.

Alan Giagnocavo
Publisher

Gretchen Bacon
Editor

Troy Thorne
Design and Layout

© 2005 Fox Chapel Publishing Company, Inc.

Chainsaw Carving an Eagle is an original work, first published in 2005 by Fox Chapel Publishing Company, Inc. No part of this book may be duplicated for resale or distribution under any circumstances. This is a violation of copyright law.

ISBN 1-56523-253-4
Publisher's Cataloging-in-Publication Data

Doeren, Jamie.
    Chainsaw carving an eagle / by Jamie Doeren and Dennis Roghair.
    -- East Petersburg, PA : Fox Chapel Publishing, 2005.

        p. ; cm.
        ISBN: 1-56523-253-4

    1. Wood-carving. 2. Chain saws. I. Roghair, Dennis. II. Title.

TT199.7 .D64 2005
736/.4--dc22   0505

To learn more about the other great books
from Fox Chapel Publishing, or to find a
retailer near you, call toll-free 1-800-457-9112
or visit us at **www.FoxChapelPublishing.com.**

Note to Authors: we are always looking for talented authors to
write new books in our area of woodworking, design, and related crafts.
Please contact Peg Couch, Acquisitions Editor, with a brief letter describing
your idea at 1970 Broad Street, East Petersburg, PA 17520.

Printed in China
10 9 8 7 6 5 4 3 2 1

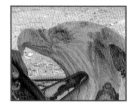   

CONTENTS

JAMIE DOEREN

Jamie Doeren is a chainsaw carver from Wisconsin. While eagles are not his all-time favorite subject to carve, he admits that they are popular with the folks who visit his shop. Aside from carving eagles with a chainsaw, Jamie also carves bears, mantels, staircases, and much more. For more information on Jamie's work, visit www.chainsawsculpture.com.

DENNIS ROGHAIR

Dennis Roghair started carving at an early age with a pocket knife, a tool he used to carve many small projects. In high school, he inherited hand carving tools by way of a brother's wife. With these tools, he paid his way through college in Utah doing sculptures while earning a degree in wildlife management. Dennis now carves full time in Hinckley, Minnesota. He can be reached there or contacted through his website at www.SculptureByRoghair.com.

Acknowledgments

Dennis: First, I want to thank my wife, Bev, who has been very patient with most projects I have tried to undertake. She has also greatly improved the carvings I have been doing through constructive criticism. When I have "finished" some of the "best" carvings I have ever done and asked her opinion, she has given honest feedback on how things could be improved. Because of her I have become a better carver than I could ever have been on my own. Thank you for believing in me. I love you.

I would also like to thank Kent Peterson, the first person I saw using a chainsaw for doing sculpture. I met him while I was attending college in Utah. He was willing to give me some pointers, and, through him, I guess I really started my life's work.

Thanks to Jamie, my coauthor and friend, for asking me to write this book with him. I don't know if I would ever have attempted to do something like this on my own. Thank you also for feedback, ideas, and methods for doing things when sometimes my own ideas have gone dry.

Jamie: I want to thank Dennis Roghair for being there when my life was sometimes too much for me. Dennis has been like a best friend and, at times, like a brother. Without him, my books would have never become reality, and this book might not have been finished. We have shared carving and life for as long as I have known him, and I will always consider him my brother and best friend.

Special thanks to my mom, Beverly Delvoye.

Both authors would also like to thank all of the suppliers listed on page 75 for their support of this project. Lastly, they wish to thank all of their fellow carvers for encouragement, support, new ideas, and the motivation to become better sculptors.

INTRODUCTION

For this book, I have teamed up with Dennis Roghair, my friend and mentor. Together we have over 40-plus years of experience in chainsaw carving. Dennis has been carving since the age of four and has contributed to all aspects of the carving sequences in this book. As you go through the book, you will notice similarities and differences in some of our techniques. We hope that our combined presentations will give you more options and styles to refer to as your ability progresses.

I've developed my style and techniques through years of failure and success, knowing that I had to be willing to fail before I could succeed. Keeping this process in mind as you carve, remember to refer back to the book when you are frustrated and to try again. The only way to get better is to keep at it. Don't worry about fixing mistakes. Finish the carving you are working on and "fix it on the next one."

For the four carvings in this book, the logical and most practical way to begin is to grab a log and rough it out with a chainsaw. The excitement grows as the shape continues to emerge from the log form. This type of carving offers many rewards in terms of physical exercise, such as spending time outdoors and close to nature in the fresh air.

We have included in this book techniques and instruction for achieving the general recognizable shape of the animal and for achieving the animal's features, using simple and straightforward methods. Your objective does not need to be to reproduce every conceivable and minute detail. Slight changes in size, pose, behavior, color, or overall general effect will correctly match the detail of the eagle being carved. You have four different projects to choose from, and you can modify them to your needs as you become more comfortable and proficient. We have also added finishing ideas and joinery.

Each carving project is accompanied by multi-view photos. Some have important techniques shown with clear, close-up photography to make it easier for you to duplicate that particular carving.

As you follow the carvings from learning the basics of the eagle's head to developing the basics of chainsaw carving to creating a soaring eagle, all you need to succeed is the willingness to try. Once your first carving is completed, the creative juices will be flowing, and other carvings will come in quick succession. As you try harder and more complex carvings, your hunger for more knowledge will grow into more and more success.

Good luck!
Jamie Doeren

CHAPTER 1

GETTING STARTED

In this section, we will explain the proper use and operation of the tools you will need for this book. Also included is information to help you choose the right equipment, wood, and finishes for these projects and future projects. The safety information in this book is general information; always read the manuals that come with your tools.

SAFETY FIRST

Fitness to Operate a Chainsaw

In general, safe use of a chainsaw calls for the operator to have a reasonable degree of both physical and mental fitness. People with disabilities need not necessarily be excluded from work with chainsaws; however, medical advice may restrict the tasks they can do and require increased levels of supervision. Prospective operators with health issues affecting mobility, alertness, strength, vision, manual dexterity, or balance should seek further medical advice before operating a chainsaw.

Conditions That May Affect a Chainsaw User's Abilities

Seek medical advice before using a chainsaw if any of these physical or mental traits are compromised.

- mobility (arthritis, stroke, etc.)
- alertness (diabetes or alcohol/drug dependency)
- physical strength (heart conditions)
- vision (unable to be corrected by glasses or contact lenses)
- manual dexterity/grip strength (vibration, white finger)
- balance (vertigo or giddiness)

Health Risk Reducers

Chainsaws expose operators to high levels of noise and hand/arm vibration, which can lead to hearing loss and conditions such as white finger. These risks can be greatly reduced by the following practices:

- purchasing low-noise/low-vibration chainsaws (anti-vibration mounts and heated handles)
- using suitable hearing protection
- keeping proper maintenance schedules for chainsaws and protective equipment
- getting proper training and information on the health risks associated with chainsaws and the use thereof
- wearing personal protective equipment

Of course, these are merely suggestions and are not meant as medical advice. You are encouraged to seek medical attention if you observe any signs or symptoms of health issues that may affect your ability to use a chainsaw safely or of adverse health effects from noise and/or vibration.

Training

Chainsaws are potentially dangerous machines that can cause major injury if they are used by untrained people. Anyone who uses a chainsaw at work should have received adequate training and should be competent in the use of a chainsaw for that specific type of work. The training should include the following general points. If you have never received any training, courses are available through most forest services or lumber producer associations in your local area.

Basic Training

Know the following dangers and precautions before using a chainsaw to create artwork:

- dangers arising from the chainsaw itself
- dangers arising from the task for which the chainsaw is to be used
- the precautions to control these dangers, including relevant legal requirements

Safe Operation

When operating a chainsaw, there are a few rules to observe before you start your saw.

1. **Choose the right saw for the job and for you.** Choosing the right saw is sometimes the most important part. If you're cutting down a 48-inch diameter tree, a 16-inch bar isn't going to go far. For the purpose of the patterns in this book, you will need relatively small saws. To choose a saw, always look at the size of the engine, not the size of the bar. The most common mistake we see is people going to a dealer and asking for a 16-inch saw, which refers to the bar size. The bar just holds the chain; the engine has to turn the chain around the bar. Every manufacturer has a book that will state which bar lengths each saw can handle. Remember, the longer the bar, the more chain there is, and the harder the saw has to work. Work with your dealer to pick the saw and bar sizes you will need for your ability and your project. We will recommend a few saws and bars later.

2. **Read the manufacturer's safety manual.** All new saws are sold with a safety and operating instruction manual. Read the one that comes with your saw. These manuals will go over all safety precautions and proper operation of your saw.

3. **Always wear protective clothing.** Protective clothing, chaps, boots, gloves, hearing protection, and eye and face protection are necessary. Dress accordingly; don't take chances. When I sold saws, I was always told, "I don't cut very often, so I don't need chaps." Wrong! The less you cut, the less you know your equipment, the greater the margin for error, and the more you need chaps. A good pair of chaps costs $60; an emergency room visit is about $350, including stitches.

4. **Maintain your equipment.** Poorly maintained equipment is dangerous equipment. Keep the chains sharp and the bars true and free of burrs. Use only proper bar oil. Bar oil is designed for chainsaw bars, and, when carving, it pays to use the best quality available to you. We recommend Amsoil Synthetic Bar Oil. Keep air filters clean, use a fresh plug, and have good starter rope. If you are not capable of maintaining your own saws, find a dealer or a good service technician who is. Get referrals, because most lawn and garden shops know little about chainsaw carving and how to repair or maintain the equipment.

5. **Use safe work habits.** Don't take risks. If you find that you absolutely have to, always think before you do. A little common sense goes a long way.

   Find a good area to work in, one that is away from buildings, roads, and curious onlookers. Use a tarp to protect you from the sun and to give you shelter from the rain. Keep your work area clean of debris. Chips and chunks of wood lying at your feet can cause a fall. Use a stump to get the carving up to a comfortable working height, and then fasten the carving securely to the stump using 3½ to 4-inch dry wall screws and a cordless drill or impact driver. To prevent a sore back, you might have to use a few stumps of different heights to keep your work at the right level. Another way to keep your work steady and at a good height is to use an old barber chair. Remove the seat and mount a piece of log on it. The log allows you to fasten your carving down. The chair base allows you to turn the carving, to raise and lower it, and to lock it in place.

TOOLS AND MATERIALS

Chainsaws

You can do all of the projects in this book with two saws. Some people choose to use one saw, switching bars and chains for each step, which we don't recommend. We will be using Husqvarna chainsaws of a few different sizes.

Husqvarna 336

We recommend the Husqvarna 336 as a detail saw. It is a newer saw and is great for detail carving. Its light weight makes it easy to handle, and the 2.0 hp engine gives it a faster speed than some of the other detail saws. We recommend a dime- or quarter-tip bar with a ¼"-pitch chain.

Overall Dimensions

Weight, excluding cutting equipment - -8.4 lbs / 3.8 kg

Cylinder displacement - - - - - -2.2 cu.inch / 35.2 cm³

Power -2.0 hp / 1.5 kW

Maximum recommended engine speed - - -13,800 mm

Fuel tank volume - - - - - - - - - - -0.76 US pint/0.36 l

Oil tank volume - - - - - - - - - - - -0.34 US pint/0.16 l

Oil pump type - - - - - - - - - - - - - - - -adjustable flow

Cutting Equipment

Chain pitch -.325"

Recommended bar length - - - - - -13–16" / 33–40 cm

Ergonomics

Sound level -99 dB(A)

Noise emissions, LWA - - - - - - - - - - - - - -112 dB(A)

Vibrations, front/rear handle - - - - -4.3 m/s² / 5.1 m/s²

Husqvarna 346XP

The 346XP is a good all-around saw. It has enough horsepower to sport a longer bar, but it is light enough to work with a carving bar. The Husqvarna 353 is another good all-around saw. It's similar to the 346XP, but the characteristics of the two saws are not identical.

Overall Dimensions

Weight, excluding cutting equipment -10.6 lbs / 4.8 kg

Cylinder displacement - - - - - -2.7 cu.inch / 45.0 cm³

Power -3.4 hp / 2.5 kW

Maximum recommended engine speed - - -14,700 mm

Fuel tank volume - - - - - - - - - - -1.06 US pint / 0.50 l

Oil tank volume - - - - - - - - - - - -0.59 US pint / 0.28 l

Oil pump type - - - - - - - - - - - - - - - -adjustable flow

Cutting Equipment

Chain pitch -.325"

Recommended bar length - - - - - -13–20" / 33–50 cm

Ergonomics

Sound level - - - - - - - - - - - - - - - - - - -100.5 dB(A)

Noise emissions, LWA - - - - - - - - - - - - - -114 dB(A)

Vibrations, front/rear handle - - - - -3.3 m/s² / 3.4 m/s²

Husqvarna 395XP

The 395XP is the ultimate saw. Even though there are bigger saws available, you shouldn't need one bigger than this. When slabbing or blocking out a large carving, the 395XP saw can make quick work of most any job. However, we do not recommend this saw to beginners.

Overall Dimensions

Weight, excluding cutting equipment -17.4 lbs / 7.9 kg

Cylinder displacement - - - - - - -5.7 cu.inch / 93.6 cm³

Power -7.1 hp / 5.2 kW

Maximum recommended engine speed - - -12,500 mm

Fuel tank volume - - - - - - - - - - - -1.9 US pint / 0.9 l

Oil tank volume - - - - - - - - - - - - -1.1 US pint / 0.5 l

Oil pump type - - - - - - - - - - - - - - - - -adjustable flow

Cutting Equipment

Chain pitch -3/8"/.404"

Recommended bar length - - - - - -18–36" / 45–90 cm

Ergonomics

Sound level - - - - - - - - - - - - - - - - - - -102 dB(A)

Noise emissions, LWA - - - - - - - - - - - - -111 dB(A)

Vibrations, front/rear handle - - - -6.5 m/s² / 10.2 m/s²

There are many more models and many different manufacturers of chainsaws. The three saws listed here are the ones we used to make the projects in this book. You can get other saws to match these specs from your local chainsaw dealer, but we only recommend the tools we use. Shindaiwa has a few saws that are smaller and easier to control than the ones we mentioned above. They can be set up with a 12-inch carving bar. Echo makes a smaller saw that handles well for beginners.

Carving Bars and Chains

On your detail saw, you're going to want a dime-tip bar and a ¼"- pitch chain. In a lot of cases, these might be hard to acquire through a dealer because many dealers are unfamiliar with carving products. For your convenience, we have listed supplies and suppliers in the back of the book for reference.

Carving bars come from a couple of different manufacturers and private makers. They come in a few general sizes: 12 inch, 14 inch, 18 inch, and dime tip. There are several other variations and lengths, including nickel and quarter tips, but these are the most common. Carving bars have a solid tip with a hard facing, which means there is no sprocket.

Chains come in different sizes as well. You can run different sizes of chains on carving bars, but ¼" pitch is our recommendation because it is smaller and you will get better detail with it.

Caution: Never try to run ⅜" low pro or .325" on a dime-tip bar; it will burn up the bar or split the tip.

WOOD SELECTION

Any type of wood can be carved with a chainsaw. Having said that, we need to say that some woods are better to use than others for various reasons. Some woods are so soft that they will not hold detail well, while others are so hard that they seem to take forever to carve.

Some woods are more susceptible to rot, which is a consideration if the sculpture will be exposed to conditions that cause deterioration.

Life-size eagle carved from white pine by Dennis Roghair. White pine was chosen because it details well and is fairly light. The eagle was hung using piano wire and was placed to seem as though it just flew in through a large window. The sculpture was finished with a clear preservative and, when sufficiently dry, was varnished and painted.

Locally grown wood

Your physical location will also determine your choice of woods. We are located in the upper Midwest and have quite a wide variety of woods to choose from. Our wood of preference here is white pine. This wood can be used for carvings that will go inside or outside. It is soft enough to carve fast, which is important if you carve for a living, but it is also hard enough to hold fine details, such as hairlines. White pine is more decay resistant than other woods, like red pine or basswood, and it takes preservatives well. Any checking is fairly predictable—usually one large check. However, white pine is not very strong, so if the sculpture will be of structural importance, such as a crosstie in a log home, we would use red pine. Red pine is stronger than white pine.

In our area, we have a wide variety of deciduous trees, including red and white oaks, elm, willow, cottonwood, box elder, catalpa, walnut, silver and sugar maples, and basswood. All of these can be carved, but woods like the maples, the elm, the willow, and the cottonwood have high moisture content. High moisture content is a problem for chainsaw-carved sculptures because of rot. Rot is caused by fungus that eats the wood. For the fungus to be active, it needs three things: wood, moisture, and a warm environment. The warmer it is and the more moisture the wood has, the faster the wood will rot. Therefore, woods that have high moisture content need to be either dried out or treated with preservatives.

To get a high moisture content wood like cottonwood to dry, your sculpture design should eliminate large masses of wood. If this cannot be done (for example, the carving is of a large eagle, and the body area is too large to dry), you should soak the sculpture with a borate solution. Borate can be obtained from log home building supply stores. It comes as a powder to be mixed with water, per the instructions on the container. It will effectively eliminate the onset of the fungus that causes rot.

Woods with lower moisture content—like the oaks—carve slower and are considerably heavy to try to move around. When these woods dry, they usually get a lot of small checks. Catalpa is a fairly soft wood that carves beautifully. The grain of this wood is also very distinct, with alternating rings of brown and a greenish color. It also doesn't do much cracking; however, it is sometimes difficult to find large pieces of catalpa that haven't rotted in the center. Walnut is also a beautiful wood. In a freshly cut walnut log, the sapwood is white and the center is very dark brown. This can be used for some dramatic effects in a sculpture. If you do an eagle banked in flight by cutting the log on a diagonal, you will have the wing tips, the head, and the tail in the white while the rest is dark brown.

If you live in the South and Southeast, some of our favorite woods there are white cypress and tupelo. In the East and Northeast, again, there is white pine. In the Northwest and western states there are western red cedar, redwood, ponderosa pine, and others.

Locating wood suppliers

To find a supply of wood in any area of the United States and Canada, you can check various places: city dumps, tree trimmers, sawmills, state and national forest services (check the government section of the phone book), and power companies (they clear trees overhanging their power lines). If you stay in one place that is visible and carve there regularly, sometimes wood will find you. We get people stopping by all the time, saying they would like to get rid of some trees. We have even had people drop off logs anonymously while we were gone.

Gluing up wood

If you cannot locate logs or trees to carve, another possibility is buying lumber and gluing up pieces of adequate size. This will work, but it involves more time and expense. If you do this, be sure to use glue that will work where the sculpture will eventually reside. An indoor piece can be glued with carpenter's glue; one that is displayed outside will need waterproof glue. If the wood you are gluing is damp, like most sculptures carved from whole logs are, a glue like Gorilla Glue will work where a water-based glue will not hold at all. Gorilla glue cures because of a chemical reaction between the glue and the moisture that is present in the log.

Minimizing cracks and checks

Everyone wants to know about cracking or checking. Can it be avoided? Probably not completely, but it can be held to a minimum. When wood dries, it shrinks in diameter. The reason wood cracks while it is drying is because it dries unevenly. The log's surface that is exposed to the sun and wind is drying faster than the inside of the log. Because the inside is protected from the elements, it stays moist and doesn't shrink. The outside, because it is drying, is shrinking but cannot get smaller because the inside isn't dry. The outside has no place to shrink down to, so it has to crack to relieve the stress. That's why a freshly cut log that is eight feet long and

twelve inches in diameter will be eight feet long and approximately eleven inches in diameter when it is dry.

Life-size eagle carved from white pine by Dennis Roghair. This eagle's wings were carved from a different log and added in because there was no log of the correct size or shape available to match the design requested. Because this eagle was to be displayed inside, a varnish finish was used to allow for easier dusting.

If you choose to carve a log that has been dried, it will have cracks already in it. Simply design the carving so that the main crack is in the back. We feel that the best approach to avoiding cracks is to carve the log while it is green, and then apply a finish that will slow the drying process, so that the sculpture can dry more evenly. If possible, we will place a cut on the center of the back side of the carving running from the top down through the base to allow the wood room to expand and contract. Other solutions are to design a piece that eliminates the center of the log, to hollow out the carving, or to glue up boards to a sufficient size. However, none of these methods are foolproof; expect some cracking.

FINISHING FOR CARVINGS

Fresh cut log

Beginning stages of mold

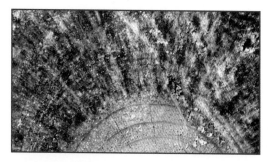

Advance stages of mold

Insect damage

When determining the type of finish to use for your carving, consider where the carving will be placed. My preference for carvings that will go outside is a wood preservative. For the carvings that end up inside, I prefer applying a varnish over the top of the preservative. For woods that have a very high moisture content or for woods that decay easily like cottonwood, willow, basswood, and elm, I think it is best to use a borate solution on the wood before sealing it.

Preservatives should have U.V. inhibiters, fungicides, a semi-transparent stain (unless you want the wood to weather gray), and a water repellent. The reasons for each of the properties are listed below; the photos at the left show the effects of mold and insect damage on untreated wood.

U.V. inhibiters help block the ultraviolet rays of the sun that cause graying and degradation of the wood fibers.

Fungicides help to stop rot and mold from happening and make the wood somewhat unpalatable to insects.

Stain gives the wood color and also helps to keep it from weathering to gray.

Water repellents are usually paraffin-based and stop raindrops from soaking into the wood while allowing water vapor to escape. A finish that lets water vapor escape is important because it will allow the wood to dry.

I suggest a régime of applying the preservative two times a year for three years, then once a year for three years, and then about once every three years. At this point, when rain no longer beads up on the carving you know it needs another coat.

If the carving is going to stay indoors, I suggest starting with a preservative, and then applying a varnish after the carving has had a chance to dry. I suggest thinning the varnish down with an equal amount of thinner so that the varnish will penetrate well. Apply coat after coat (waiting the required time between coats) until the varnish finally stays on the surface, not soaking in. Finish off with an unthinned coating of the varnish.

TYPES OF CUTS

In this section, we'll look at some of the basic chainsaw cuts and their uses.

Angle Cut

The saw is held to make a cut that is some degree between horizontal and vertical. This cut is usually used while blocking out or roughing in a carving to take off large chunks of wood. These cuts are also called sloping cuts.

Curving Cut

A curving cut follows the contour of part of the carving. It can either penetrate the wood slightly, as it would in laying out feather groups, or go completely through the log to block in an area of the carving.

Horizontal Cut

This cut is parallel to the ground. Use horizontal cuts to block out an area. Shallow depth horizontal cuts are used for tasks such as laying out an area for a bench seat.

Piercing Cut

A piercing cut is a plunging cut, where the tip of the saw is pushed into the log. This type of cut is used for blocking in areas when pushed all the way through the log. Shallow piercing cuts are for laying out areas.

Smoothing

Lay the bar flat against the wood and raise one side of the bar slightly. With the other side of the bar touching, sweep across the surface of the wood. Use this technique to create smooth surfaces.

Sweeping Cut

Run the saw at a high rate of speed and sweep it across the wood surface. The angle of the bar determines the width of the swept-out area. For instance, if the bar is perpendicular to the ground, the cut will be only as wide as the chain.

Texturing

Texturing is done using the tip or the tip's edge to add lines of detail to a carving.

Veining

Veining is a type of texturing cut that makes the surface of the wood look like the surface of a feather. Drag the saw bar sideways on the wood surface to create this cut.

Vertical Cut

A vertical cut is a piercing cut that is vertical to the ground. This cut is used for various areas in the carving, such as the leg.

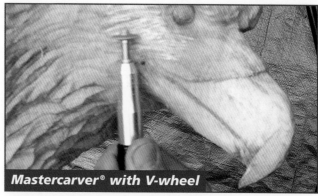
Mastercarver® with V-wheel

OTHER TOOLS

The tools shown in this section may be useful to you as you are refining your chainsaw sculptures.

Here, Dennis is using the Mastercarver Pro flex-shaft with a twist-lock hand piece. The Diamond V-wheel works well for doing fine feathering lines on the face. With this tool, you can obtain finer detail than is possible with the chainsaw alone. Because the tool is reversible, cuts can be easily made with the grain of the wood to prevent fuzzing.

Mastercarver® with Diamond Bur

The small pointed diamond bur with the Mastercarver Pro is used to carve in the eagle's nostril. It also works well for adding the detail around the eye.

Angle Grinder

An angle grinder with sandpaper is useful in smoothing the beak.

Wood Hog

Eye Tool

The Wood Hog, when set up with an eye tool, is used to make the eyes. While eyes can be made with a chainsaw alone, using this tool makes things much easier. It makes a perfectly round eye and, because of the high speed of the tool, the eye is polished smooth. This polished surface will make the eye shine when a finish is applied.

CHAPTER 2
CARVING AN EAGLE'S HEAD

Jamie designed this project because he always had scrap wood lying around that looked like a wedge. It was too big and too nice to throw away, so he had to come up with an idea to use it. This simple pattern doesn't take very long to carve. If you can get the detail in the head right, the rest comes easily. Jamie used a Husqvarna 336 with a quarter-tip bar and ¼"-pitch chain to carve this project. He added color to the eagle with white, brown, and yellow spray paint.

TOOLS AND MATERIALS

- **WEDGE SCRAP OF WHITE PINE**
- **DETAIL SAW (HUSQVARNA 336) WITH QUARTER-TIP BAR AND ¼-PITCH CHAIN**
- **TWP CEDAR-TONE WOOD PRESERVATIVE**

1 Cut the bottom of the wedge, so the wood sits straight on the base.

2 The first cut is a curved cut. It will form the back and the top of the head. This cut can be done in one cut.

3 The result.

4 Next, make the cut that forms the top of the beak.

5 Angle cut to remove a wedge-shaped piece of log. This cut will maintain the wedge shape of the original log.

6

The result.

7

Mark where the beak and brow meet by making a cut that will serve as a stop cut.

8

This cut sets the angle of the beak. The beak doesn't have to be perfect yet. This is just a preliminary cut.

9

The result.

10

Use a sweeping motion to gouge out an eye socket.

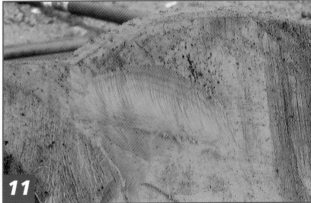

11

The result.

12

This next cut sets the length of the beak. Remember, you can always make the beak shorter, but you can't make it longer. Be sure to study your reference material to get the proportion correct. (See page 73 for photos to get you started.)

13

This piece needs to come out of the way. Make sure you maintain the beak angle. It's narrower at the tip and wider toward the head.

14

Remove the piece under the beak to form the neck. You don't have to remove it with one cut (I'll use two), but it should be easy enough to do with a dime- or quarter-tip bar. You should be able to see the roughed-out head now.

15

The result.

16

Smooth the cut using the tip of the bar. Round the cut toward the front so that there are no square corners on the neck.

17

Mark the separation between the beak and the head.

18

Put in the line that separates the beak from the raised area, where the nostrils are located. Check your reference material for correct placement.

19

The result.

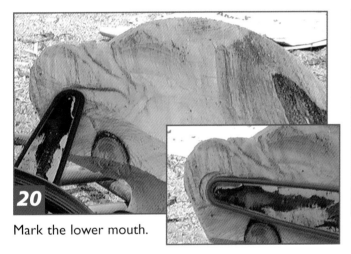

20

Mark the lower mouth.

21

The result.

22

Cut up to separate the jaw and the beak.

23

Remove the excess wood from the bottom jaw.

24

The result.

25

Trim and round the neck.

26

Smooth the beak.

27

Detail and trim the lower jaw.

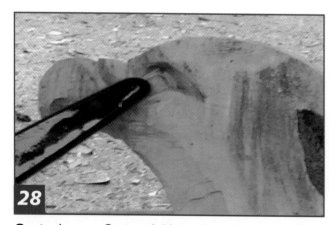

28

Cut in the eye. Option: Additional detail can be added later, at your discretion, with a die grinder.

29

Clean up the rest of the log and remove the bark.

Do a final trimming of the neck. Notice how the bark has been cleaned off the sculpture.

Begin texturing the top of the head where the head meets the beak. Pay attention to the grain, so the texture won't fuzz out. Don't carve against the grain, as it will cause chipping and fuzzing.

Continue texturing along the side of the face below the eye.

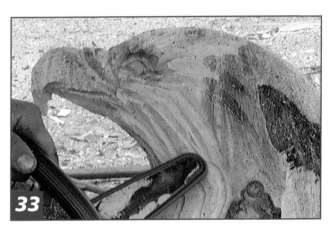

Add texture along the neck.

Texture a little deeper on the back of the head.

Cut through in some spots on the back of the head to make it look like the feathers are raised.

36

The results.

37

Take a thin layer of wood off, so the surface is uniform for lettering.

38

With the tip of the saw, make two parallel lines to mark the height of the letters. Try to keep the lines at least four inches apart so the lettering can be seen from a distance.

39

Make perpendicular lines to create boxes for the letters. For "Welcome" you need seven boxes, one for each letter. I try to make mine a little curved to add some uniqueness to the look of the letters.

40

Trim around the blocks at an angle. This will give the blocks some depth and make them look like they are sticking out farther than they really are. Now, just write W - E - L - C - O - M - E.

41

The final sculpture is ready for finishing.

CHAPTER 3

CARVING AN EAGLE WITH A FISH

This project is a basic perched eagle; however, Dennis added a fish in the talons and rotated the head of the eagle to the side to create a more interesting carving. These two details can change a stiff-looking bird into a more realistic-looking bird, having the appearance of motion.

TOOLS AND MATERIALS

■ ONE LOG, 3' BY 14" IN DIAMETER

■ ROUGH-IN SAW (HUSQVARNA 346XP)

■ DETAIL SAW (HUSQVARNA 336)

■ ANGLE GRINDER TO SAND THE BEAK

■ WOOD HOG WITH EYE TOOL

■ STAINS AND PRESERVATIVE

Place the log on the stump.

Secure the log to the stump with screws. We use 3½"-long RSS Fasteners. These fasteners cut into the wood without needing a pilot hole. A star-shaped bit drives them in, and they have a built-in washer that gives them tremendous holding power. (From GRK Fasteners—see the Resources section on page 75.)

The first cut is about five inches deep and sets apart the head area. The cut is made approximately one-third of the way in from the left edge of the log. This log was roughly 15 inches in diameter, so the cut was placed about five inches from the left edge. This cut will lie by the right side of the eagle's head and beak.

Make a piercing cut at an approximate 45-degree angle to remove wood from behind the head and above the back.

Another piercing cut is made at a slightly steeper angle to slope the lower part of the back.

6 Take off the block of wood.

7 Remove the wood from the chest area and in front of the legs, making a sloping cut in, then a vertical piercing cut, then a horizontal cut in.

8 Remove the block below the tail of the eagle.

9 Working with the chest area facing you, make the cut that will be the back side of the head; then make the cut above the shoulder to remove the block behind the head.

10 Remove the block of wood above the beak and in front of the forehead.

11 Make the cut that forms the front of the beak and remove the block.

12 Two angled cuts make the wedge-shaped beak.

13 At this point, the eagle is blocked out. Now, round the upper edge of the back to the shoulder.

14 Round the square corners on the head next. Start by rounding the beak.

15 Round the top front and the top rear of the head.

16 Round the top of the beak.

17 Next, round the top of the head.

18 Make a cut below the beak and above the shoulder.

19 Continue to round off more square corners on the head.

20 Cut the sides of the wings.

21 Make the cut in the center of the back where the wings meet.

22 Cut a wedge of wood where the wings taper down to the center cut.

23 A shallow cut marks the front edge of the wing.

Cut from the breast side, marking the outline of the chest area. This cut meets the preceding cuts on the wing, done in Step 23.

Remove the wedge-shaped block of wood that makes the wing area stand out.

Make the same series of cuts on the other wing area.

Round out the edges of the chest area.

A shallow cut to the side of the head moves the head area back a little. Looking at the top of the eagle in Step 29, you can see how the head is set back just a bit from the chest area.

Make a curving cut to round the chest area.

Round the wing area.

The area of the wing is thick enough to carve the wings opened from the body.

Round the chest area.

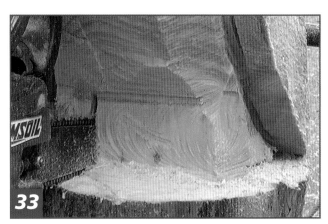

Make two vertical cuts (one here and one on the right) to set out the inner leg area.

Tip the chainsaw upside down so you can make a cut that follows the chest/belly contour between the two leg cuts.

Make a horizontal cut at the base of and between the leg cuts. This cut should meet with the cut of the chest contour and will release the block between the legs.

36

Block out the feet by first making horizontal and vertical cuts between the two feet.

37

Remove the wood.

38

Remove a block of wood in front of the left leg (on our right in the photo).

39

Make a similar series of cuts to the outside of the right foot.

40

The right foot area is now blocked in.

41

Begin to block out the fish with a vertical cut and a curving cut.

The result.

Make two more cuts on the opposite side of the fish.

Continue roughing in the fish by making two horizontal cuts to separate the fish's body from the base.

A vertical cut marks the head of the fish.

Remove a chunk of wood here as shown.

Remove a triangular-shaped piece of wood to finish blocking the fish.

48

Block in the top of the left foot.

49

A side view of the foot shows the curving cut that follows the contour of the foot. This cut continues to the base to relieve the fish.

50

Additional cuts are made to bring out the fish.

51

Make cuts beneath the fish to bring the fish out from the block.

52

Turn the eagle around and begin working on the lower area of the feathers.

53

Lay out the lower edge of the secondary feather group.

Round the secondary feather area.

Undercut the area under the secondaries.

The carving at this point.

Lay out the primary feather group of the left wing.

Cut around the sides of the primaries to give this area a raised look.

Lay out the right primary feather group. Notice that on this project we decided to have the left feather group cross over the top of the right primary feather group.

Relieve the right primary feather group, leaving that area raised.

Remove wood from the left and right sides of the tail feathers to block out and raise the tail area.

Make angle cuts on both sides to slope the edge of the tail feather area.

Check your progress against these photos of the carving to this point.

Remove the block of wood to the outside of the left leg above the foot.

Make cuts behind the leg for the removal of wood from this area.

66 Make a piercing cut from the front left of the leg to the back to release the block of wood behind the leg.

67 With the tip of the chainsaw, dig out more wood between the back of the legs.

68 At this point, go back to the head for detailing. First, round the head.

69 Narrow and round the beak; then carve in the depression where the eyes will be with the tip of the chainsaw.

70 Contour the face area with sweeping cuts. Choose the angle for the bar based on the look you wish to achieve. For example, holding the bar at a 45-degree angle will give you a gouge cut that's roughly ¹⁵⁄₁₆" wide.

71 Notice the small cut centered above the beak area. This is where the feathers of the forehead radiate from.

72

Round off the front edge of the beak. Then, draw a centerline that you will shape the beak down to, so that the beak doesn't have a flat front surface.

73

Shave wood off the beak to the centerline. If you look closely, you can also see the raised area to the right of the beak where the nostrils are located.

74

Cut in the lower edge of the upper beak on both sides. At this point, if you don't feel confident enough to do the somewhat delicate work of carving an open beak, just shape the underside of the beak to create a closed beak and move on to Step 77.

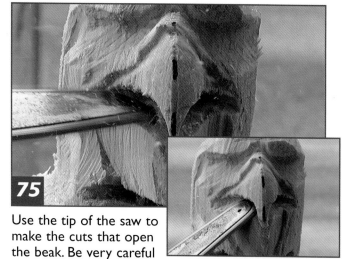

75

Use the tip of the saw to make the cuts that open the beak. Be very careful here so as not to clip off the tip of the beak.

76

With the tip of the chainsaw, make cuts to the side of and under the tongue.

77

Detail the underside of the beak.

78

Sweeping cuts from beside the eye to below the beak further shape the face area.

79

Detail the feathers on the head with the saw. To do this, the saw chain is spinning and the edge of the chain is then touched to the wood, moved slightly, touched again, moved again, and so on. Do the entire head in this manner. The feathers flow from the beak toward the back of the head and down.

80

Continue texturing the front, top, and back of the head.

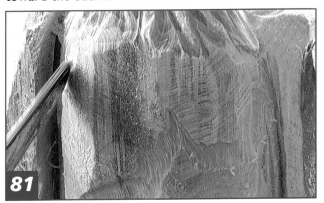

81

Texture the breast, the underside of the wing, and the belly area with the saw tip. Lay one side of the bar tip against the wood and, with a slight up-and-down shaking of the saw, sweep over the surface of these areas.

82

Round the leg.

83

Add feather texture to the leg. This texture is done with a very shallow piercing-type cut.

Smooth the surface of the wings before adding the feathering. To do this, lay the bar flat against the wood, and then raise one side of the bar just slightly away from the wood, leaving the other edge against the wood. Sweep the edge of the bar across the surface of the wood. Repeat as necessary.

Carve a slight indentation behind the shoulder area. What appears to be the shoulder is actually the wrist. The indentation is the area between the wrist and the actual shoulder, and it runs down to the elbow.

Lay out the area for the second row of feathers. This cut is done on both wings.

Undercut this area with a shallow cut.

Follow the same process for a third row of feathers. Do this on both wings.

Add individual feathers to each of the rows using the side of the saw tip. Be sure to make your cuts with the bar lying close to the surface of the eagle. The feathers in the second and third rows are set so that the feather to the rear is on top of the feather in the front. Do both wings.

90

A closeup of the feathers on the bird's right wing shows the texturing effects. Lines, or veins, on each feather must run in the correct direction as shown.

91

To put in the veins, hold the saw upside down so the chain cuts in an upward movement, giving a clean cut to the wood.

92

The second row of feathers on this wing is almost complete.

93

Start on the third row of feathers. Notice that this row overlaps in the opposite direction and has no line on top for a border.

94

Detail the upper edge of the wing where it meets the wrist (what appears to be the shoulder). Hold the saw upside down again and cut in the feathers with the edge of the tip. The feathers are carved in order from the bottom to the top.

95

Texture the area between the wrist and the third row of feathers by moving the tip of the saw in a shaking/sweeping motion. Do this on both wings.

96

The completed wing area.

97

Cut the feathers on the primary area. The top feathers in this area overlap the lower feathers. Do both wings.

98

Undercut the wing where it overhangs the leg area. Do both wings.

99

Undercut the tail area to a depth of about two inches on the right.

100

Undercut between the stump and the tail feathers on the left.

101

Lay out the center tail feather.

102 Cut away the wood beside the center tail feather to place this feather on top of the underlying feathers.

103 Texture the central tail feather.

104 There are 12 tail feathers on an eagle. When the eagle is perched, the center feather is on top with five feathers dropping to one side and six to the other. Cut in the successive tail feathers.

105 The feathers on the left side are almost complete.

106 Remove a triangle-shaped piece of wood in front of the right leg to give the leg a bent-back look.

107 Begin the texturing of the leg.

108

Clear out some wood behind the fish and the legs.

109

Lay out the toe area on the leg holding the fish.

110

Shape and detail the head of the fish.

111

Cut in the eagle's toes. These are the toes that grasp the fish.

112

Add some detailing to the fish.

113

Cut in the lower fin by the fishtail.

114

Shape the fish's tail, and then add some vertical lines with the tip of the saw to show detail.

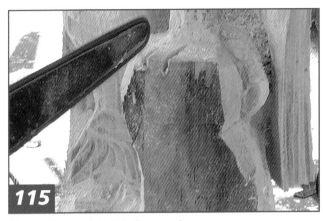

115

Carve the eagle's left foot and toes.

116

Remove the wood from between the toes to raise the foot area. Detail the tops of the toes.

117

Shape the sides of the toes, and then curve the bottom of the talon.

118

Carefully shape the talon and remove wood so it stands free from the base. Finish the other toes in a similar manner.

119

Undercut the fish.

Shape the stump on which the eagle is perched.

Make a knothole in the stump.

Continue to shape the stump under the fish's tail.

The completed stump.

Creating Eyes
To create the eye on this eagle, I lay my chainsaw aside and pick up a Wood Hog. I made a tool from a bolt especially for carving eyes. (See Step 124.)

Cut and burn the detail for the eagle's eyes using a bolt modified for this purpose or a similar tool.

Sand the beak with an angle grinder.

Apply finish to the completed carving. We used a cedar-colored wood preservative with brown stain for highlights.

The completed carving.

CHAPTER 4
CARVING AN EAGLE BENCH

The cuts made for the eagle bench are very similar to those made for the Eagle with a Fish sculpture. The major differences are that the bench eagles are sitting much straighter and that the base has a notch cut to hold the seat.

In this carving, Dennis carved two eagles for the bench ends. Both eagles have their heads turned in opposite directions, so that they are looking away from the center of the bench. He ripped a separate log in half, with a slab ripped off for the seat and the back. The inside wings are carved into the seat back.

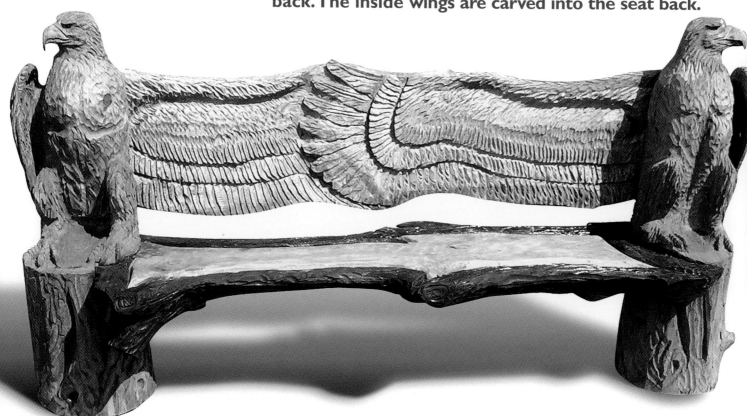

TOOLS AND MATERIALS

- TWO LOGS, APPROXIMATELY 4' LONG BY 16" IN DIAMETER FOR THE BENCH ENDS
- ONE LOG, 6' LONG BY 20" IN DIAMETER FOR THE SEAT AND THE BACKREST
- LARGE ROUGH-IN SAW WITH A 2' BAR (HUSQVARNA 395XP) FOR SLABBING THE BENCH AND BACK
- MEDIUM ROUGH-IN SAW (HUSQVARNA 346XP)
- DETAIL SAW (HUSQVARNA 336)
- ANGLE GRINDER TO SAND THE BEAK

Measure up 18 inches from the base of the log. Make a level cut approximately 2 inches deep for the top of the seat area. This cut can be seen in Step 4 close to the bottom center of the photo.

Block in the head. Notice that the head area is blocked in to the back center of the log. In this photo, I have already removed the wood to the left of the head and am now removing the right piece of wood.

Cut the back of the eagle's profile. Notice that the cut below the head area is quite vertical. This area forms the surface where the backrest of the bench will be attached.

Cut the profile of the breast area.

Two piercing cuts make the knee/leg profile.

A third piercing cut makes the top of the foot. Notice the horizontal cut below the foot. This cut forms the top of the seat area.

Make a cut under the area where the beak will be. This will release the block from the front of the eagle. Then, remove the block from the front profile.

An angled cut removes wood from the back of the head.

Cut a notch marking where the head meets the beak. Then, cut the excess from the front of the beak.

Remove the piece from the top of the beak.

Make the cut that forms the outside profile of the bird's right wing.

The left body area is blocked out. The inside wing will be added later.

Make a sloping cut for the wing/shoulder area. Continue downward, removing just the bark and rounding out the log. Note that this is the right back side of the right wing.

Make two cuts, each approximately one inch deep, to delineate the wing area on the eagle's right side.

Make a horizontal cut at the base of the tail, about 8 inches up from the ground.

A sloping vertical cut allows the removal of the block of wood below the tail.

Remove the bark from the base. Notice the shape of the finished cut under the tail as completed in Step 16.

Remove the bark and round the left side of the bird.

Make two vertical cuts to open the right wing from the body. Remove the wood between the cuts.

Cut away the corner on the eagle's left side to round the chest.

Make two vertical cuts to block out the leg area.

Make a horizontal cut to finish the leg area.

Round the chest by removing the hard corners on the left and right sides of the eagle.

24

Taking out the block between the legs requires several cuts. The first cuts are triangular in shape.

25

Another triangular shape is cut from the remaining wood between the legs.

26

The result is a triangular-shaped body between the two legs.

27

Slope and shape the back and top of the wing.

28

Mark the center of the back where the wings come together.

29

Slope the right side into the center cut to shape the wing.

Remove a block of wood on the left side to open that area for the insertion of the left wing.

The project to this point as viewed from the back.

The project to this point as viewed from the front.

Make a number of small cuts around the head, knocking off the sharp edges and shaping the head.

Using the tip of the bar, take several passes to carve a trough for the eye.

Round the area between the beak and the face with the tip of the bar.

Separate the face from the back of the head with a sweeping cut using the tip of the bar.

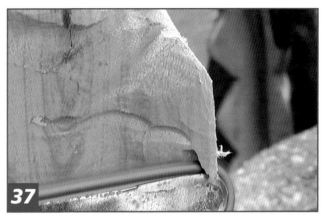

Undercut the hook of the beak as shown. (The detail on the beak will be added in Step 40.)

A piercing cut marks the bottom of the beak. Be careful to keep the hook intact.

Remove the wood under the beak.

Add detail to the beak. A wavy line shows the opening of the beak, and a diagonal line separates the face from the beak.

Remove the rough corners from the face area.

42 Use the tip of the bar to add feather detail to the head.

43 Finish detailing the head.

44 Add feathers and detail to the neck and chest area.

45 Round the belly and separate the toes on the eagle's right foot.

46 Round and detail each toe.

47 Cut a notch under the eagle's left foot, and then separate and detail each toe.

48

The progress to this point.

49

With the tip of the bar, draw the two lines marking the feather locations on the wing.

50

Add feather details between the lines.

51

Add feather details to the shoulder and to the top of the wing.

52

Add feather details to the back.

53

Undercut the bottom of the wing.

Add lines to mark the long feathers at the bottom of the wing.

Continue the feather detail on the back of the wing.

Smooth the area under the tip of the wing.

The tail falls below the shelf where the seat back will rest. Outline the tail with the tip of the saw; then remove the wood around it to relieve it from the base.

The tail has been blocked in.

Blend the top of the tail into the body.

Add texture to the top of the tail.

Cut in the long tail feathers on the bottom of the tail.

Remove the wood to the side of each tail feather to make it look like one feather overlaps the next.

The finished tail.

This photograph shows the notch under the left foot where the bench seat will be inserted. Notice how erect the eagle stands.

This six-foot-long log will be the seat bench and seat back. Rip it in half with the large rough-in chainsaw.

Rip a three-inch-thick slab from half of the log. The slab will be the wings. The round part of the log will be the seat.

Prop up the log for the seat, so that one end of it rests next to the notch below the left foot.

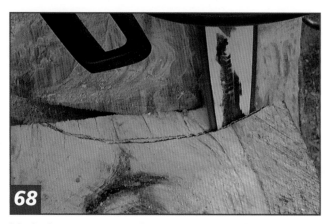

Mark the contour on the seat; then cut the log to the contour mark.

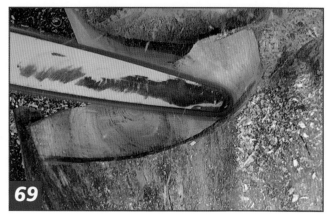

Flip the seat over and cut a tongue on the end of the log to fit into the eagle base.

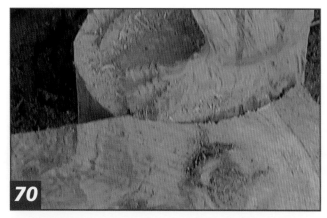

Flip the log over and place it next to the base of the eagle again.

This photo shows the underside of the seat. Mark the base where the tongue will be inserted.

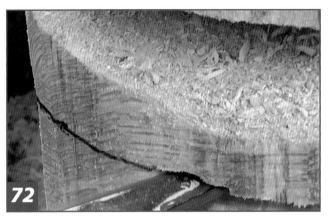

Cut in at the line to make the notch for the tongue.

Clean out the notch by removing small chunks of wood at a time.

Shape the notch to receive the tongue of the seat bench.

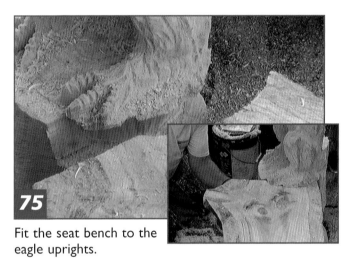

Fit the seat bench to the eagle uprights.

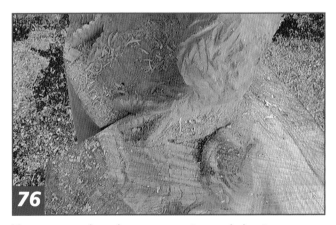

You may need to do more cutting and shaping to get a good fit.

The three-inch-thick slab that was cut from the log in Step 66 is now fitted to the back of the eagle uprights to form the backrest.

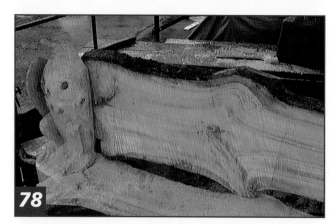

78

From the front, the backrest should appear to be the eagles' extended crossed wings.

79

Fasten the seat back to the eagle upright with three six-inch screws or lags. We used 6" RSS Fasteners because they have superior holding power, they won't strip out, and they will not rust. (From GRK Fasteners—see the Resources section on page 75.)

80

Finish the assembly of the bench and draw lines for the wing areas.

81

Cut the wing edges. Relieve the wing area in the center so it looks like the wing from the eagle on the left side of the bench (right side of the photo) overlaps the wing from the eagle on the right side of the bench.

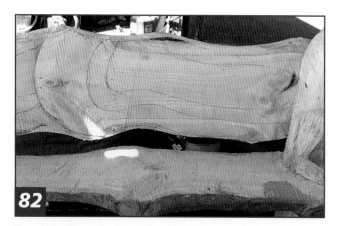

82

Draw in the main feather groups.

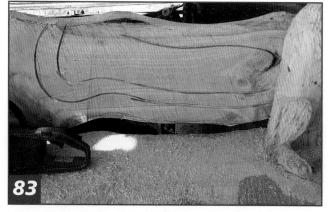

83

Make shallow cuts for the feather groups.

84

Remove wood from the outside of each of the cuts so that the feather groups on the top of the wing are layered on top of the other feathers.

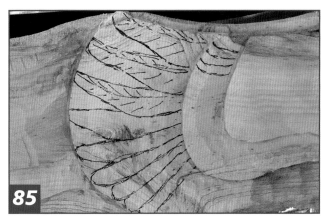

85

Draw in the first nine primary feathers (there are 10 total) and start to draw in the primary coverts. The first three primaries show the direction of the feathering lines.

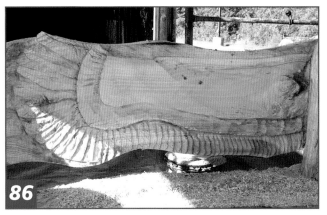

86

Carve the primaries and secondaries. Note that the feathers on the underside of the wing are carved so that the outside feathers overlap the feathers closer to the body.

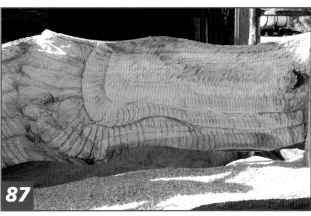

87

Continue to carve in all of the feathers on the underside of the wing.

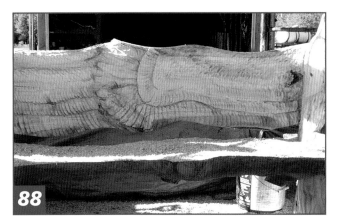

88

All of the feathers have been carved on the underside of the wing.

89

Detail the feathers on the back of the seat back. Notice that from the back, the opposite eagle is overlapping its feathers.

90

Decorate the seat bench so that it looks like the seat has a border of logs.

91

To show some contrast on the seat, paint the "logs" on the seat bench with brown spray paint. They could also be stained.

Finish the bench as desired. This one was finished with cedar-colored stain and a wood preservative.

CHAPTER 5

CARVING A SOARING EAGLE

This soaring eagle project is one that Dennis did a long time ago when he carved at shows. The balance of the project is what caught Jamie's eye, and, through the years, he has tried to duplicate the balance that he always saw Dennis achieve with many of his sculptures. Be sure to pay attention to the base and the size of the eagle, making sure the eagle weighs less than the base or it will not stand. Learning to use this type of balance in your projects will help you to develop your own style of projects that are stable but amaze the viewer's eye.

TOOLS AND MATERIALS

- ONE LOG, 12" TO 14" IN DIAMETER AND 5½' LONG
- DETAIL SAW (HUSQVARNA 336) WITH QUARTER TIP BAR AND ¼"-PITCH CHAIN
- ROUGH-IN SAW (HUSQVARNA 353) WITH 16" BAR AND ⅜LP CHAIN

Start with a log approximately six feet tall and 14 inches in diameter.

Make a diagonal cut through the log.

You should have two almost-identical pieces when you are finished.

Find the center of the log by measuring the length and dividing by two. This will help you in placing the head.

Make a rough sketch of the eagle's body, a little bigger than the actual size of the finished sculpture. This sketch will act as a guide to keep you from removing too much wood. Use the centerline to help keep both wings the same size.

Remove the back piece. This cut should be parallel to the first cut, but it will run only three-quarters of the way down where a cut will be made in from the outside edge.

The piece to this point.

Following the sketched-in lines, start removing the outer pieces. I start at the head for the first cut.

Then, I make two angle cuts defining where the head area and the tip of the beak are.

The result.

Remove the area behind the head.

Cut the top wing. Stay wide of the lines so you don't remove too much wood at once.

Now cut out the bottom wing. I cut just a little at a time on the bottom wing because it starts into the base.

Continue to cut the very bottom of the wing. Don't cut too far into the base.

Remove the wood below the bottom wing so the wing appears to be relieved from the base.

Make angle cuts on both edges of the tail.

Take out a piece of wood to give the wings some movement, so the wings don't look too straight.

Trim off the excess wood, rounding the front and back of the wings.

Remove wood from the top wing to create motion here as well.

A side view of the piece at this point shows the concave shape of the wings.

Take the top wing down to the right thickness (approximately 3 inches so that you can have room for feathers on both sides) and shape. Remember, you don't have to trim it down exactly on the first pass. Don't remove too much too fast.

Trim the front to keep the shape of the wing.

Trim the tail.

24

The result.

25

On the back of the sculpture, cut the tail and blend it to the body and wing.

26

Remove the excess from the inside of the tail. This step also helps to shape the rear part of the body.

27

Trim and thin the inside of the wing.

28

The result.

29

Thin the head and part of the wing.

Remove the inside of the lower wing.

Shape the body and the breast.

Trim and shape the tail section.

Blend the body and the wings.

A look at the underside of the sculpture from the side.

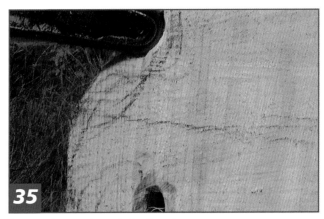

Shape the neck and the head.

Rough out the head.

Shape the beak.

Draw the feather groupings.

Carve the feather groupings.

Scoop out the wing tips using the tip of the saw. This will give the wings the look of movement. I set the eagle on its side to do this.

Draw in the individual feathers. Notice the effect of the scooped-out wing tips.

42

Carve the individual feathers.

43

Shape the wing to its final size and proportion.

44

Define the edge of each feather.

45

Thin the wing by removing the back portion of the wing.

46

The result.

47

Take the excess wood off the back of the body and the wing, and then blend the body into the wing.

48

Cut the underside of the wing away from the stump.

49

Carve the feathers on the top wing. Again, I've set the eagle on its side to do this. It is always a good idea to find a way to work that is easy on your back and arms.

50

Remove the excess wood on the top wing.

51

Define each feather on the top wing.

52

The result.

53

Draw the feather groupings of the top side of the lower wing; then carve and define the individual feathers.

54 Cut away the excess wood from the stump to define the wing tip.

55 Cut away the excess wood from the surface of the tail to reduce the depth of the tail.

56 Carve and define the individual feathers on the tail.

57 Carve feathers into the head and the neck.

58 Carve feathers into the back of the body.

59 Cut away the excess wood from the underside of the tail and carve the individual feathers.

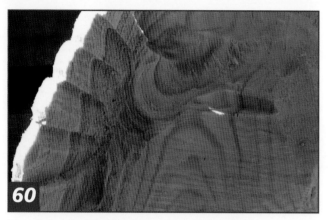

Blend the underside of the tail to the body.

Trim the excess from the underside of the wing.

Blend the underside of the body to the wing.

Cut away the excess wood from the underside of the body.

Carve the feather groupings on the underside of the top and bottom wing.

Carve the individual feathers on the underside of the top and bottom wing; then blend the wing to the underside of the body.

Cut away the excess wood of the stump on the underside of the bottom wing.

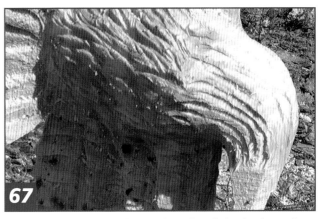

Carve feathers into the underside of the body and the neck.

Shape the top of the head and the open beak.

Cut the base. Keep in mind that too much of an angle will not support the eagle if you don't have a large enough base. If you make a mistake, you can add wood to the base with glue or by using drywall screws.

Cut away the excess of the base.

Shape the rocks on the back of the base.

Shape the rocks on the front of the base.

The finished soaring eagle.

Photo by Bob Mead. Taken ½ mile from Dennis Roghair's home.